A PRACTICAL GUIDE TO

RUNES

SIMON LILLY

Acknowledgments:

Photography: Charles Walker Photographic; p. 6, 9 and 89

S&S Lilly; p. 3, 4, 5, 7, 8, 10, 11, 17, 34, 35, 43, 48, 52, 68, 72, 81,

87, 91 and 96

Published in 2002 by Caxton Editions

20 Bloomsbury Street

London WC1B 3JH

a member of the Caxton Publishing Group

Designed and produced for Caxton Editions

by Open Door Limited

Rutland, United Kingdom

Editing: Mary Morton

Typesetting: Jane Booth

Digital imagery © Photodisc inc.

Title: A Practical Guide to Runes

ISBN: 1 84067 299 4

A PRACTICAL GUIDE TO

RUNES

SIMON LILLY

CAXTON EDITIONS

CONTENTS

INTRODUCTION

T he runes appeared as a magical alphabet during the Early Medieval
Period of Northern Europe, the so-called Dark Ages. Each rune, made
up of straight lines, represented a letter, a facet of human experience and
a spiritual energy. Although used in later centuries as an alternative to the
Latin alphabet, the runes seem to have been originally formulated for
divination and magic.

Above: runes on the 7th century Anglo-Saxon Franks Casket, which shows a hunting scene within a border of runes.

Up until a couple of decades ago knowledge of the runes was almost exclusively the province of scholars and linguists studying the Medieval and Dark Ages in Northern Europe. A resurgence of interest in divination and mysticism during the 1960s and 1970s kindled a desire to know more about home-grown belief systems, but over and above this, the phenomenal success of J.R.R. Tolkien's *The Hobbit* and *The Lord of the Rings* stirred the imagination of a whole generation. Although works of fiction, these books drew heavily on Tolkien's main areas of study, Anglo-Saxon and Old English literature, which were themselves rooted in the shared mythology of the Northern European peoples. The original cover to *The Hobbit* included rune inscriptions that translated into modern English. It became a new secret code for some, a symbol of the mysterious magic of our ancestors to others. But there were difficulties for these new runic enthusiasts. Original, primary documentation on the runes is very thin on the ground. There are relatively few archaeological artefacts scattered across Europe that have rune inscriptions upon them – mainly objects of stone and metal. Apart from a brief and rather inconclusive mention concerning a method of divination amongst the Germanic tribes in *Germania* written around 120AD by the Roman war correspondent cum historian Tacitus,the earliest written evidence of runes and rune use is the *Anglo-Saxon Rune Poem*. Ironically this record of a 9th-century Christian monk only exists in an 18th-century copy which was made by an antiquarian shortly before the original document was lost in a fire. The next oldest document is again a copy, the original of which was written around the beginning of the 13th century. Known as the *Old Norse Rune Poem*, it describes in

evocative but abstruse imagery the meanings of the 16 runes of the Scandinavian system. Finally, the *Old Icelandic Rune Poem* was written down about the beginning of the 15th century and again described in truncated imagery the 16 signs of the Scandinavian runes. Other references to runes and rune use are scattered throughout the Icelandic sagas of the Early Middle Ages.

Below: a 9-card sample of rune cards.

INTRODUCTION

Below: the methods of rune divination owe much to methods of casting objects onto the ground and interpreting the fall in terms of the desired answer.

Whence, then, did our current systems of using the runes derive? Certainly the methods of rune divination owe much to methods of casting objects onto the ground and interpreting the fall in terms of the desired answer. This is a worldwide method of divining oracles and must be very ancient indeed. The gods or spirits involved affect the outcome of the diviner's cast, creating significance and meaning out of random chance.

Another way of rune reading today owes more to the pre-arranged patterns and spread of tarot and card divination. Here, each place in the pattern has a designated meaning that the randomly selected rune defines and describes.

A fundamental difference between using runes and other methods of divination is that the runes not only have particular meanings but also specific magical powers. Runes have stronger historical roots in the world of magic and so can be used both for indicating the future (divination) and also for encouraging a change of outcome (magic). Despite the fact that rune knowledge has only survived to the present day by the thinnest of threads, its inherent practicality and flexibility has gone a long way to encouraging new and valid research and exploration.

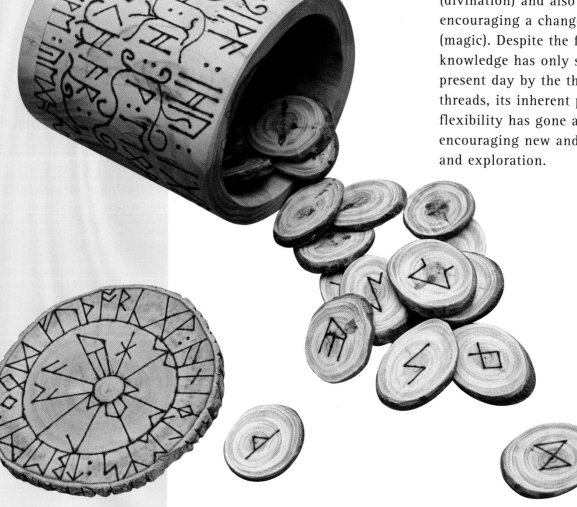

Despite the certainty of some scholars, there is no clear evidence for the origin of the runes. There are some similarities to other early alphabets like the Italic script and Etruscan alphabets of Northern Italy, but there are also similarities to symbol pictures dating from the Neolithic period some 5,000 years earlier.

In the end it seems to come down to whether the ancient peoples of Northern Europe are thought of as savage barbarians, in which case a Mediterranean origin will be favoured, or as noble tribesmen, in which case an indigenous invention is preferred. Nationhood and national boundaries are a very modern invention. Migration, trade, war and disasters all play important roles in the spread of ideas and the creation of new concepts. Perhaps, as some suggest, the runes emerged complete in the mind of a single ancient Northern seer to be passed on secretly from teacher to pupil. Perhaps the contact with other peoples who employed alphabets and writing spurred some innovators to formalise and standardise an already existing set of magical signs and symbols.

Below: a naked Nordic witch carrying rune boards inscribed with the magical alphabet. Migration, trade, war and disasters all play important roles in the spread of ideas and the creation of new concepts.

Above: originally, runes were cut into wood in such a way that they would stand out against the grain of the timber..

Far right: in 9th-century Northumbria the rune alphabet was expanded further to 32 runes, or four complete aetts.

Sweden was the last country in Europe to formally adopt Christianity as the State religion in the 16th century. Over 3,000 large stones can still be seen carved with rune inscriptions. These stones are nearly all simple memorials or boundary markers made during the Viking period (10th to 13th centuries AD). They use the last variation of the rune alphabet consisting of only 16 letters. By this time in Northern Europe, the runes had been adopted as an alternative written script to Latin. Although popularly ascribed to the Vikings, the runes are much older and belong to the forests of Germany, the North Sea coastlines and to Anglo-Saxon England. Nor do the runes naturally belong in stone. The shapes themselves clearly indicate that originally runes were cut into wood in such a way that they would stand out against the grain of the timber.

'Rune' in many old European languages has the meaning of 'secret', 'mystery', 'whisper', 'incantation'. The oft-quoted lines from the *Havamal* where Odin, the shaman god and warrior of the North, sings of a self-sacrifice hanging on the World-Tree where after nine days he 'took up the runes ... very strong staffs, very mighty staffs ... given by the great gods ... and carved by the highest kings', reflect this sense of mysterious power, of scarce-contained magical energy.

The runes considered to be the oldest are known as the Common Germanic Futhark or Elder Futhark. (Futhark names the sequence of letters F.U.T.H.A.R.K., in the same way as the Roman alphabet reflects the first letters of the Greek system: Alpha, Beta). The Elder Futhark consists of 24 individual rune symbols or staves, divided into three groups of 8 (called 'aetts').

Although many variations in drawing appear from region to region, the rune rows always follow the same order of characters.

When Germanic people crossed the North Sea and took up residence in England alongside the peoples of Celtic descent five more runestaves were added onto the existing 24 to accommodate changes in speech patterns and religious context. These 29 runes make up the verse descriptions of the *Anglo-Saxon Rune Poem*. Finally in 9th-century Northumbria it was expanded further to 32 runes, or four complete aetts. Although the earliest examples of an Elder Futhark rune row come from 6th-century Sweden, the largest proportion of surviving rune inscriptions from Scandinavia and Iceland date from the 10th century onwards and use the 16-rune alphabet.

With the tightening up of Church power across Northern Europe during the Middle Ages, rune use declined except in folk and peasant magic and in the keeping of agricultural almanacs.

BEGINNING TO USE THE RUNES

Learning to identify and remember the meanings of the runes can be a daunting task unless their underlying logic is understood.

Above: the main measure of wealth in a pastoral society was how large a herd of cattle one possessed.

The first key to unlocking the meaning of the runes is that each runestave often has a pictographic element: it resembles, in a very simplified form, the object it is named after. This can help us to remember the key energy of each rune. Thus the first rune, FEOH, which means 'wealth', resembles the head and horns of a cow – the main measure of wealth in a pastoral society was how large a herd of cattle one possessed. Some runestaves are a lot more pictographic than others, but it is usually possible to link the shape with a relevant object. BEORC, for example, means 'birch tree', but the runestave looks like an angular capital B – not really anything like a tree. However, the idea of mothering and nurture associated with the rune suggests the form may represent a mother's breasts.

The second key, which can prove even more useful, is the actual shape of each runestave. At first glance the runes look like a random

Visually the vertical line is static and stable. There is no sense of movement or dynamism. On the other hand, the diagonal line

Left: each runestave represents a blending of two fundamental polarities of energy, ice and fire, or stillness and movement, contraction and expansion and so on.

arrangement of straight lines. Breaking down each into its elements reveals that the whole system is devised from two basic types of line: the vertical (|) and the diagonal (\ ).

The simplest of all the runes in shape is called IS ('ice'), which is a single vertical line (|), and CEN ('fire/torch') which has several variations of shapes, the most easily identifiable being two diagonal lines meeting together to make a 'V' shape on its side (<).

suggests instability or change and is dynamic. Using this analysis, it can be seen that each runestave represents a blending of two fundamental polarities of energy, ice and fire, or stillness and movement, contraction and expansion and so on. Looking to see whether a runestave possesses more of one sort of energy than the other and seeing whether it is balanced, symmetrical and steady or not gives a good clue as to the sort of energies represented.

Above: the concept of wealth and abundance that FEOH represents has a strong element of "use it or lose it" – the correct management of resources.

FEOH, for example, has two dynamic diagonals and one vertical. Placed at the top right of the upright, the diagonals look unbalanced and top-heavy. If it were to be built in three dimensions, this runestave would fall over! It has no symmetry or balance. This clearly suggests FEOH is a very dynamic energy, something that cannot be controlled or kept still. And true enough, the concept of wealth and abundance that FEOH represents has a strong element of "use it or lose it" – the correct management of resources.

In this book the Anglo-Saxon names of the runes are used. This is because there is greater differentiation between how the names look and sound than in the names derived from the Old Germanic rune names.

When you begin to work with the runes learn to associate the name with the shape of the runestave. The shape will suggest the energy it represents and the pictographic elements. The world of today is quite different from the Dark Ages of Northern Europe so, although the

ᚠᚢᚦᚨᚱᚲᚷᚹᚺᚾᛁᛃᛇᛈᛉᛊᛏᛒᛖᛗᛚᛜᛟᛞᚠᚢᚦᚨᚱᚲᚷᚹᚺᚾᛁᛃᛇᛈᛉ

energy behind each rune remains the same, the activities and objects that it represents will often have changed. It is of limited use to interpret the runes in ancient terminology, talking about the gods of our ancestors, unless these concepts can be made relevant to the world of the questioner. Divination is, after all, supposed to provide clarity and a way out of confusion, not create more obstructions!

The greatest difficulty most people have in beginning divination is the ability to bring together the information received in a meaningful way. Divination is a dynamic process. For every reading the factors are completely unique and so will be the solutions. The diviner has to combine the learned meanings within the context of the questioning. To make an analogy with painting, each rune is like a colour. Colour can be modified in tone and shade, but always carries the same basic type of energy. One colour put next to another will change the appearance of each. Even harshly contrasting colours can be blended together to create a harmony. Likewise each rune has a broad range of meanings, which the diviner should learn to blend with the runes around it. This takes practice, but is easier when it is understood that it is the diviner's mind, the diviner's intuition, that

makes sense of the symbols in front of them. Other people's interpretations, other people's methods, are at best only indicators. Intuition reveals itself in leaps and the sudden revelation of patterns, rather than the steady logical build-up of interpretations following laid-down rules and meanings.

Below: one colour put next to another will change the appearance of each.

Familiarise yourself with each rune by choosing one at random each day. This rune will be the most relevant and appropriate energy for you. To integrate with the energy, visualise the runestave in the sky in front of you as large as possible. With a long in-breath, imagine drawing that energy into your body so that it completely fills you.

Making notes about the rune and your experiences that day can help you understand the energy better.

Another useful exercise is to select a rune to work with and, taking a moment to settle your thoughts, imagine a gate or doorway. Upon the surface of the door visualise the rune you wish to explore. As you move through the door all that you experience will be related to the energy of that rune in some way. After a few minutes return back through the door and close it behind you. Make notes of your experiences. Using this as a regular exercise can really help to clarify how a rune energy can manifest in different ways in life.

Below: to integrate with the energy, visualise the runestave in the sky in front of you as large as possible.

A single rune can easily be chosen at random to sum up the energies of the moment, but most questions are quite complicated and, for a beginner, it is usually much easier to interpret the information given by a selection of three or four runes. Select beforehand what each rune place will represent. Three runes are often chosen to represent the past, present and future. Equally, three or four runes can be chosen to indicate a sequence or progression of events forward from the present situation: this is now; this will change to this; then this, and so on.

The runes themselves can be visualised as 'the whispers of the universe', primal energies, or states of energy with which humans are very familiar. As such, rune energies are present everywhere at all times. What objects the diviner chooses to use in order to represent these energies is a personal matter of taste and practicality. Traditionally each runestave will have been cut or carved onto small sticks of wood or slivers of bone. The common misconception that divining runes should be carved on stone has no archaeological basis at all. These days commercially produced rune sets tend to be ceramic or plastic. Wooden and metal rune sets can also be found. Rune cards, similar often to tarot cards in design, are also more common now. It is simple to make your own set of runes from sturdy cardboard, ice-lolly sticks or twigs.

Above: rune cards, similar often to tarot cards in design, are also more common now.

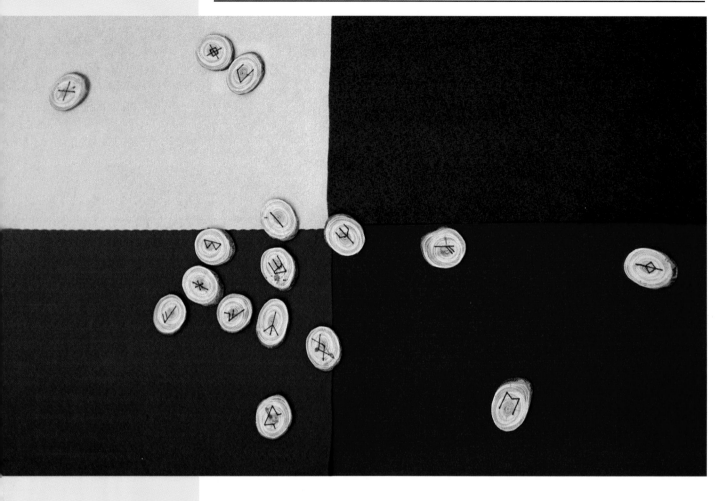

Above: all runes can be cast onto a cloth. Some casting techniques suggest an area divided into different sections, each representing different aspects of the answer.

What type of runes you have will determine to some extent how they can be used. Cards are best suited to layout readings where each one is selected from a shuffled deck. Smaller runes of wood, stone or ceramic can be kept in a bag from which they can be picked at random and then laid out in appropriate patterns.

Alternatively, all runes can be cast onto a cloth and those that land face up can be read as the answer. Some casting techniques suggest an area divided into different sections,

each representing different aspects of the answer. When runes land within an area they represent significant events there.

Different methods will suit different people. The only useful divination methods are the ones by which you are able to enter an intuitive, timeless state of mind and offer real help to those who seek advice. It is a good idea to try as many methods as you can. You will soon find those most suited to your own way of working.

EOH, pronounced 'fee', is the first rune of all the rune rows. It represents the letter 'F' and means 'cattle'. The runestave symbolises the head of a cow, grazing with its head down on the ground, horns in the air. The fact that the head is only represented here reflects some of the underlying concept of the rune. The phrase 'head of cattle' is still used to denote the number and size of a herd. How big a herd is owned denotes status and wealth. The bigger the herd, the more opportunity the owner has to acquire other goods, power and influence. So FEOH carries the meaning of wealth, abundance, ability to increase and prosper. The nature of FEOH's energy is inherently unstable. Wealth cannot be simply accumulated without energy exchange; cows cannot be kept in one field forever. The concept of energy management, husbandry – the careful manipulation of one's assets to avoid stagnancy and standstill – is inherent in FEOH.

Below: the phrase 'head of cattle' is still used to denote the number and size of a herd.

met, a cow, Audhumla was created. Licking the salt from the ice, Audhumla created the first gods and men. FEOH therefore contains an aspect of profound creativity, supporting universal life in the same way that domesticated cattle supported every aspect of the pastoral tribe's lifestyle. Magically, FEOH suggests impetus for change, a dynamic fiery energy towards increase, expansion and growth.

In divination, runes can appear the right way up or upside down. Not all readers take the orientation of a rune into account, but it does allow for a greater subtlety of interpretation. An upright rune can then be interpreted in a positive context, while if it is reversed a more difficult aspect is indicated. In a cast reading, runes can also be on their sides. If you choose to, these runes can be seen as neutral, neither favouring the positive nor negative aspects.

FEOH: cattle, wealth, abundance.

Acquisition of wealth; looking after what has been gained; opposition successfully overcome. Reversed: frustration; failure; wasting energy; what is gained dwindles; delay.

Above: FEOH suggests a dynamic fiery energy towards increase, expansion and growth.

Mythologically and magically, FEOH represents Audhumla, the first living thing. Where the two cosmic polarities of ice and fire

UR is the second rune of the first aett, representing the letter 'U'. The runestave takes the form of the body of the European wild ox or auroch, with its high, powerful shoulders. Where FEOH is the power of controlled energy, UR is the strength of untamed Nature. There are classical descriptions of an auroch hunt where young men would attempt to prove their courage and strength by killing a trapped animal – a dangerous business.

Linguistically, UR relates to many words and concepts to do with primal energy, beginnings, fate and vitality. It is uncontrollable, primitive, a surging life-force, the energy of Urd, the Mother Earth Goddess herself.

Below: the horns of the docile Highland cattlke are a pale reflection of their fierce ancestors, the auroch or wild ox of Europe.

The shape of the runestave can be seen as an auroch or as a fountain or geyser erupting forcefully from the ground. It can also represent a gateway, a change from one state to another that requires courage and strength to pass through. When UR appears in a reading there is great potential for growth, but opportunity needs to be taken 'by the horns'. Unless risk is taken, we don't know how capable we are.

The meaning of UR will vary depending on the area being examined. It can represent one's own physical vitality and health – the amount of raw life-energy we possess. UR can also indicate the need for courageous action and perseverance against the odds.

Magically, UR suggests primal, raw, life-energy – the means to begin, to continue and to change our lives.

UR: auroch (wild ox), vitality.

Power; strength; ability to face all challenges; opportunities for change and taking up new responsibility.
Reversed: missed chances; failure of nerve; low energy; lack of self-confidence; fear of change and the unknown; bad luck.

THORN is the third rune of the first aett. The sound it represents is 'TH' as in 'thorn'. The rune means 'thorn' and the stave represents the same. The second main image relates to the god Thor, half god, half giant. The Germanic name for this rune is 'Thurs' or 'Thurisaz', meaning giant.

Thor was one of the most popular of the Norse gods among the ordinary people. He represented the power of the fertilising rain, particularly the thunderstorm, and was the protector of both the gods and mankind against the malevolent giants. The runestave can be seen as Thor's hammer, his weapon that, when thrown at an enemy, would always return back to his hand.

Far left: the shape of UR can represent a geyser erupting forcefully from the ground.

Below: Thor was one of the most popular of the Norse gods among the ordinary people.

Below: magically, THORN suggests a strong defensive space.

Both these images, the thorn bush and the god Thor, sum up the energies of this rune. A thorn bush is both a danger and a stronghold, defensive and offensive, depending on where you are. For someone hiding from harm the interior of a thorn bush is a safe place to be, difficult to reach without injury.

However, for one who has fallen into a patch of thorns, attempting to get oneself out will usually only make things worse. In a difficult position only the help of another, more experienced person, can bring a resolution.

Against the might of strong, outside forces ('giants'), only a strong defender ('Thor') can be of use. THORN indicates a need for care and good advice. Correct focus and application of energy will be needed to succeed.

Magically, THORN suggests a strong defensive space, a protection from all harmful influences. It also refers to focussing energy on a desired end, like a hammer driving in a nail.

> *THORN: a thorn, caution.*
>
> *Important decisions require guidance; move carefully; protection; self-protection; unexpected help; setback. Reversed: extreme caution required, do nothing; wait for help; be flexible.*

OS is the fourth rune, which means 'mouth' and represents the letter 'O'. In the Elder Germanic Futhark this rune is called ANSUZ and is the letter 'A'. In the Anglo-Saxon rune rows, however, the sound value changes and other runes are used as 'A'. Both represent aspects of the same energy – the flow of communication – though in the Anglo-Saxon runes a differentiation can be made between mundane, ordinary levels of speech, and the speech of inspiration and divine guidance.

OS relates to the Aesir, the sky gods of the Norse pantheon, and especially their leader Odin or Woden, patron of warriors and the shaman, magician and seer. It was Odin who discovered the runes whilst hanging from the World-Tree, an ash.

Below: OS relates to the Aesir, the sky gods of the Norse pantheon.

THE RUNES

OS is the flow of breath, inspiration, information, the passing on of knowledge and even wisdom. It is also chatter, gossip, the unwanted influence of others and misinformation, depending on how the rune appears in a reading.

Magically, OS represents the freeing up of energies. Like helpful information or like the wind itself, OS suggests a release from constricting circumstances, blowing away cobwebs to bring inspiration, literally 'the breath of life'.

In a divination the appearance of OS suggests that attention should be given to what is being said and what is being heard (not always the same thing!).

OS: mouth, communication.

Information; news; messages; learning; wisdom from unexpected sources; elderly or knowledgeable persons.
Reversed: mischief; gossip; misinformation; nothing is what it seems; interference from superiors; refusal to learn.

Below: In a divination the appearance of OS suggests that attention should be given to what is being said and what is being heard (not always the same thing!)

RAD is the fifth rune of the first aett. It represents the letter 'R' and means 'riding'. In all the rune poems RAD has the same flavour – that is, it's all very well dreaming about riding out like a hero into the world, but the reality is usually much more immediate, uncomfortable, wet and cold. The runestave can be visualised as a horse's head and forelegs stepping out, or as a person taking a step – the first of a long journey, perhaps.

RAD has a connection not only to journeys and roads but also to solar energy, the sun's disc, the wheel of the horizon, the directions and so on. The form of the runestave suggests this relationship in the similarity of the zigzag diagonal with the solar rune SIGEL, one simply mirroring the other.

Above: the runestave of RAD can be visualised as a horse's head and forelegs stepping out.

Below: RAD can sometimes indicate a physical journey of some kind.

RAD can sometimes indicate a physical journey of some kind, but more often it represents the energy needed before setting out – a sense of motivation, of urgency and focus, a quest. RAD refers to the way, the path in the sense of finding one's own direction and purpose for starting a new activity. It counsels, 'Don't just sit there planning endlessly. Get up and do it!'. Practical exertion, perseverance in the face of difficult conditions, focusing attention on the desired goal without distraction– these are all contained within this rune's energy. A useful mnemonic is to see the runestave as someone getting 'a good kick up the R's'.

Magically, RAD concentrates energy into a powerful focus before allowing it to release outwards towards the desired goal. The rune also emphasises personal resolve, one's own path in life.

RAD: riding, action.

Action is preferable to words; time to broaden experience; short journeys; the Right Path. Reversed: delays; bad, difficult paths; learning the hard way; boasting.

CEN, sixth rune of the first aett, means 'torch'. There are several variations of shape to this runestave. One frequently found is a single diagonal line either rising or sloping down from the centre of the vertical line, much like the letter 'K', which is the alphabetical sound of this rune.

A torch is a means of illumination, which in olden days was made from pinewood dipped in resin or pitch. Some say the runestave represents the stands upon which the torches were fixed to light rooms and passageways. CEN suggests light illuminating darkness, removing shadows – it reveals the truth and imparts knowledge. The runestave can be seen as an eye that sees, the light of knowing, the clarity of comprehension. To 'ken' is 'to know' in Old English and North British dialects. 'Cunning' derives from the same root, as does 'kenning', the poetic skill of creating complex allusion and metaphor to impart, but also conceal, knowledge.

Below: CEN suggests light illuminating darkness, removing shadows – it reveals the truth and imparts knowledge.

Above: as fire, CEN can also be destructive.

As it is connected with fire, CEN can also be destructive. It appears in the Norse and Icelandic poems in the form of an ulcer – that burning wound in flesh so difficult to heal. CEN, though, is mainly considered to be a creative, initiating energy. It can indicate a desire for learning or can sometimes represent desires of a more lusty nature!

Magically, CEN is the energy of wisdom, the revelation of the truth, the source of any real power. As a fire rune it stimulates and activates, bringing clarity and dissolving darkness in its many forms.

CEN: torch, creativity.

Creative energy; positivity; strength; power; transformation; health; knowledge.
Reversed: loss of prestige and social standing; loss of belongings; limitations; stagnancy; ignorance; untruth.

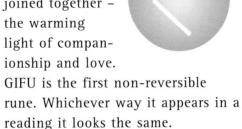

GIFU, pronounced with a hard 'g' and short 'i' , like in 'gift', is the seventh rune of the first aett. It means 'gifts' and 'giving' and represents the complex interactions that such activities engender. Its sound is the hard 'G' as in 'good'. GIFU is unique amongst the runes as it is still in use today with its original meaning. The kisses at the bottom of love letters are simply this rune of love and friendship!

The runestave can be seen as two people kissing each other on the lips, or as arms crossing over each other as gifts are exchanged. GIFU is two CEN runes joined together – the warming light of companionship and love. GIFU is the first non-reversible rune. Whichever way it appears in a reading it looks the same.

Below: the runestave of GIFU can be seen as two people kissing each other on the lips.

Below: the Anglo-Saxon lord's gifts of gold and honour supported all those around him.

The context of this rune will decide its meaning. In the area of relationships, partnerships and love it represents a harmonious and balanced exchange of energy – mutual appreciation, mutual feelings. GIFU is always an energy of relationship of one to another, and the need to maintain a balance of responsibility.

For any gift is a bond created between the giver and the receiver. The oldest Indo-European root words from which it derives are 'ghab' and 'gheb'. As with many root words, these two contain the opposite core concepts both of giving and taking – for in truth it isn't possible to do one without the other act also being present. Gift-making and the act of generosity were an integral part of many tribal cultures. The Anglo-Saxon lord was patron of culture, keeper of peace and commander of warriors. His gifts of gold and honour supported all those around him. To have one's lord's patronage withdrawn made a person an outcast without means of material support, protection or status.

Magically, GIFU is connected with all works of love and where an equal and open exchange of energy is required.

GIFU: gifts, giving.

Giving; responsibilities; obligations; partnerships; generosity; love; friendship; unity of action and intention; feeling at home in the world.

WYN means 'joy'. It is the eighth rune in the first aett, representing the letter 'W'. The runestave is said to symbolise a banner blowing in the wind or a weathervane. WYN derives from the same root as 'wind', 'to win', 'winsome' (meaning attractive) and 'Venus' and possibly also the 'Vanir', the tribe of Earth-based gods of fertility and joy who became the Elder Ones in Asgard alongside their allies the Aesir, Odin, Thor and so on. The Aesir seem to represent the religious development focusing on the warrior sky-god, away from the older, pastoral religion focused on the earth-goddess. The Aesir and Vanir initially were mutually suspicious and, although they seem to have kept to their separate camps in Heaven, did eventually live peacefully together. From the tales that remain it seems much of the powerful magic acquired by Odin came from the Vanir.

This quality of togetherness, of harmony belongs to the rune WYN. The banner or flag identifies the group, the clan, the family – those who feel happy together in mutual support and power.

In divination, then, WYN suggests a light, airy joyous energy where there is a sense of achievement, a bringing together and strengthening of related things. Magically, WYN represents the power of the will. Like the wind itself, the will is invisible yet can, when focused enough, remove all obstacles in its way. Even a gentle breeze can eventually bring about completely different conditions in the weather.

WYN: joy, harmony.

Joy; happiness; transformations for the better; will and power; enthusiasm; encouragement. Reversed: unhappiness; grief; loss of affection; disparate energies.

Below: like the wind itself, the will is invisible yet can, when focused enough, remove all obstacles in its way.

This is the first aett, sometimes called Freya's or Frey's aett. Freya and Frey (literally 'The Lady' and 'The Lord') are the chief deities of the Vanir, the old fertility gods of Northern Europe.

Looking at these eight runes we can see certain visual patterns emerge. There is only one rune, GIFU, which is non-reversible. In fact, GIFU is completely symmetrical about every axis. It is a dynamic form, but very stable. Five runes FEOH, UR, OS, RAD and WYN have no symmetry and so display a very dynamic, moving energy. Three runes,

THORN, RAD and WYN have enclosed areas in their forms, whilst all the other five have open forms. In all, Freya's aett has dynamic, expansive, outward-directed energy. The energy of creativity, growth and flow. The second aett shows a very different set of characteristics.

Below: the first aett - Looking at these eight runes we can see certain visual patterns emerge.

Above: HAEGL, pronounced 'hail' is the first rune of the second aett.

HAEGL, pronounced 'hail' is the first rune of the second aett. Its letter is 'H' and its meaning is the hailstone. It has been suggested that the image the runestave represents is a snowdrift between trees. In the *Anglo-Saxon Rune Poem* the qualities of this rune are defined in terms of everyday experience. Hail is a dense white grain that falls from heaven, which gets blown about by the wind and eventually turns to water. As a sudden storm the hail is destructive, damaging crops, bringing cold, preventing people from continuing their normal lives. Yet eventually it melts to water and fertilises the land once more, becoming beneficial and life-sustaining.

The sky – its rain, thunder and storms – belongs to the Aesir gods and HAEGL has become associated particularly with Heimdall, the guardian of Bifrost, the Rainbow Bridge between Asgard and Middle Earth, the world of gods linked with the world of men.

Far right: NYD has been seen as a firestick where the friction between two sticks sparks fire that will sustain life.

Below: magically, HAEGL symbolises the seed of the universe containing everything in its potential form.

Magically, HAEGL symbolises the seed of the universe containing everything in its form. It is the world of elemental forces that can crystallise into form at one moment and flow through both time and space. HAEGL refers to the laws of Nature and also the force of Nature against which no creature can stand in opposition.

HAEGL represents in divination an unexpected turn of events, something unplanned that appears to dash any hope for achieving future goals, and yet, in time, this turns out to be for the best. HAEGL always suggests a need to accept what has happened, to go with the flow, not to try to go against the inevitable changes that make up life. Accepting that the force of the Universe is greater than any individual's wishes, relax into the experience of the world as it is. HAEGL is a powerful rune of transformation and healing. A stubborn, rigid energy can melt, illness and disease can be purged, stagnancy can be driven away – but the progress will be wild and unrelenting – much like a hailstorm.

HAEGL: hail, transformation.

Disruptive natural forces; disruption of plans; apparent setbacks that eventually resolve for the better; lack of personal control.

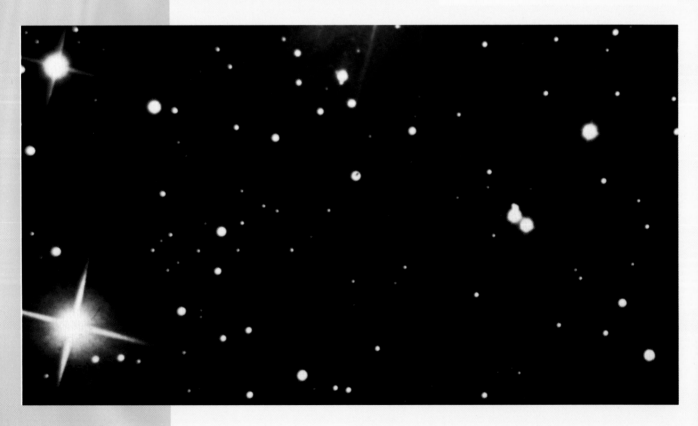

NYD, pronounced 'need' and meaning the same, is the second rune of the second aett.

It is the equivalent of the letter 'N'. The key concept is necessity – a thing that needs to be done whether pleasant or not. There is in this rune the connection with compulsion to act, craving and lust as well as the idea of duty, restoration of balance, and appropriate activity. NYD is related to the Indo-European root word 'kn...' 'to press, knead, push, bind'.

NYD is circumstance, the coming together of factors that requires specific actions, which may be difficult or unpleasant in themselves and yet will render benefit to all.

The runestave can be seen as a knot, a binding together of opposites (the vertical line of |, ice, with the diagonal cross of \, fire). It has also been seen as a firestick where the friction between two sticks sparks fire that will sustain life. Fire is a necessity for life and yet it must be bound – controlled and limited – else it becomes all-consuming. NYD requires appropriate responses and, until they are fulfilled, discomfort and disharmony will continue.

Below: NYD can loosen or it can bind.

The key to need is that, although an unpleasant experience, in itself it will stimulate action to bring an end to itself in the attainment of the desired goal.

In divination, NYD is simple. It requires that action be taken, that solutions be found. Nothing will move until the energy of NYD has been transformed. Magically, NYD ties and unties. It can loosen or it can bind – but it will always tend to act in accordance with the web of creation, the knots of interacting forces that allow things to exist and allow things to dissolve again.

NYD: need, necessity.

Caution; wait and see; patience; act appropriately; do what is needed rather than wanted; deliberate action focused over time; perseverance; duty; fears, anxiety that needs sorting out.

IS is 'ice', the letter 'I', the third rune of the second aett. IS is uncompromising. It is frozen matter with all flow suspended, self-contained and unchanging. The form of IS can be seen as an icicle. It is the simplest of runes, a single vertical line, visually stable, unmoving with no dynamic potential. In Northern cosmology ice is one of the polarities of existence, the opposite of fire. The combination of the two brings about life, but each one untempered by any element of the other is inimical to living beings.

As an energy the rune IS is more difficult to deal with than CEN or FEOH. Fire energy, though dangerous, is inherently dynamic and changing. Fire encourages creativity and movement and it needs fuel to exist. Once the fuel is exhausted, fire must move on or die. Ice, on the other hand, simply is. It requires no food other than its own lack of temperature to continue forever in its frozen state. An IS energy state is much more difficult to escape because all energy must come from outside oneself.

Above: the form of IS can be seen as an icicle.

Below: there is a linguistic and conceptual relationship between ice and iron.

There is a linguistic and conceptual relationship between ice and iron. Both are cold to the touch, but both can 'burn'. Both ice and iron hold their form and are bright, hard, implacable.

Because we are creatures of action, the energy of IS is often uncomfortable and unwanted. However, a great deal of human energy is expended in running away from things we would rather

not face when it is often better to be still, understand and resolve our problems. The energy of the rune IS holds things as they are, in uncompromising clarity and stillness. In this respect IS can seem to be clear as crystal (*krystallos* being the Greek word for 'ice'), revealing what is real and what is ephemeral.

On the other hand, IS is the solidification of energies into a rigid form that might mask what is really there underneath. Sense of self, personality, persona and how we would want to be seen in the world – in other words the ego – are also represented by IS. Magically, IS represents a focus, a holding and 'freezing' energy. It can 'take the heat' out of any aggression or disruptive force.

In divination, IS will reveal either its clarifying qualities or the frustration of lack of movement, depending on the context and surrounding runes.

IS: ice, standstill.

End of activity; wait, do not act; disagreements; things stay the same; cooling of a relationship; focus; clarity; stillness.

Below: sense of self. persona and how we would want to be seen in the world – in other words, the ego – are also represented by IS.

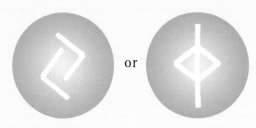

or

GER is the fourth rune of the second aett. The soft 'g' makes the rune rhyme with 'year' and corresponds to 'J' in the alphabet. GER means 'year', harvest, the passage of time and, as such, is a striking contrast to the previous rune IS.

Below: Indo-European roots for GER are 'ger' to gather, 'gher' – to grasp.

There are two main forms of GER. In the Anglo-Saxon rune rows the stave is a central upright passing through a diagonal square. This stave can be thought of as a picture of the world turning on its axis, measuring time, or as the three main faces of the moon- waxing, full and waning, or as a seed sprouting. The Germanic form is two interlinking, but separate V-shapes, which can be seen as sickle and plough , the two ends of the agricultural process.

Indo-European roots for this rune concept are 'ger' – to gather, 'gher' – to grasp, to enclose, 'ar' – to fit together. Garden, an enclosed (safe) space, that is guarded by clear boundaries, comes from the same roots, whilst from 'jera' and 'ger' derive our words 'hour' and 'year'.

GER is the rune of the cycle of time, where everything appears and changes in due season. It is a favourable rune of fertility, growth and eventual harvest, but time is the most important factor here. Things just cannot be rushed. Everything is accomplished in the right time and place. Patience and watchfulness are needed and, in the case of unwise actions, GER indicates that it is not possible to escape from the consequences of past activities.

Left: GER is the fourth rune of the second aett.

Below: an impatient farmer who digs up his seeds to see how much they have grown will never harvest a good crop.

In magical workings, GER refers to 'ripening' of events. It is not a fast-moving energy, but will bring things to a fruitful conclusion at the right time and place.

In divination GER marks time. Success will come in time. Goals will be reached in time. GER suggests that appropriate actions are done only at appropriate times. For example, an impatient farmer who digs up his seeds to see how much they have grown will never harvest a good crop!

GER: Year, Harvest.

Growth; regeneration; endings and beginnings; reaping what has been sown; plans succeed in their own time.

EOH is pronounced 'yew' and represents that tree. EOH is the fifth rune of the second aett, and has a sound equivalent to a short 'E', not a long 'eee' sound, but probably closer to the sound made by the mouth at the end of saying 'yew'. The 'eo' sound is also given as an equivalent. The stave suggests a spinning energy, static but at the same time dynamic – a good description of the rune energy itself.

The yew tree has a powerful presence in folklore and myth. An evergreen tree, living seemingly forever – and certainly individual trees are alive now that are probably over 6,000 years old – and yet producing a poison so notable that our word 'toxin' derives from the name the Greeks gave to the yew tree: *taxos*. So yew is a tree of life that can bring death, yet ironically one of its main chemicals, taxol, has been found to be a powerful destroyer of cancer cells. It is also a tree of death, commonly found in churchyards and made into deadly longbows, yet it has the ability to spring into life again when to all outer appearances it seems long dead.

Below: the yew tree has a powerful presence in folklore.

THE RUNES   45

EOH is related to Uller, the god of the yew grove and patron of hunting who was able to survive in difficult conditions. The bow was both a defence against enemies and wild animals and a means to gather food.

Magically, EOH is a powerful protective rune. It also implies great energy to enliven, resuscitate and encourage new projects.
In divination, EOH can be a warning to guard your energies from draining situations. Difficult situations may begin to show some positive movement. Very often EOH represents a time where energy must be given a chance to develop.

EOH: yew tree, hope.

News from the past; recurrence of old problems; defence against danger; all will turn out for the best; hope; survival; a quiet situation will awaken to life again.

Below: the bow was both a defence against enemies and wild animals and a means to gather food.

Below: most commentators interpret PEORTH as a dice cup or gaming piece.

PEORTH is the sixth rune of the second aett. Standing for the letter 'P', its exact meaning and symbolism is still in question. Two main concepts that are closely related are commonly accepted.

The first problem with PEORTH is that it doesn't seem to have a clear literal meaning in any language. Most commentators interpret PEORTH as a dice cup or gaming piece. In this reading the runestave can be said to resemble the cup itself or someone crouching down, hand raised to play their turn. Another reading suggests that the *Anglo-Saxon Rune Poem*, the only source of information on thus rune, was slightly modified either accidentally or intentionally when copied, changing the participants from female to male.

In this alternate reading the verse is not about gambling and drinking, but about woman giving birth – only a change of three letters in the text will create this interpretation. Now the runestave is the newborn child or the woman herself giving birth.

Whichever interpretation is favoured, the key concept of this rune is the uncovering of new things, the play of fate bringing new elements onto the scene, hidden mysteries revealed, underlying patterns of the universe glimpsed in events.

The foetal position that this runestave symbolises is echoed in the bound, sacrificial victims found drowned in bogs across Northern Europe. Evidence suggests that these ritual murders were propitiation to the deities in time of need. There are also divination techniques where the shaman is bound tightly before he/she is able to visit the spirit world seeking answers. There is a mysterious line between birth and death, ignorance and knowledge, that this rune energy enfolds.

PEORTH in magical workings highlights deep, hidden potential. It is associated with beginnings, openings, revealing. In itself it represents the deep well of the unseen worlds.

PEORTH: mystery, secrets.

Hidden knowledge; surprises; subtle changes; help; secrets and plans revealed; potential. Reversed: unpleasant surprises; disappointments; devious intentions; concealment.

Above: PEORTH can represent a newborn child or the woman herself giving birth.

EOLHX, or EOL-SECG, is 'eel-sedge', or 'eelx', the seventh rune of the second aett. Its letter is 'X' or 'Z'. The Anglo-Saxon runes associate the symbol with a strong, sharp-edged swamp grass – eel-sedge, whilst the Germanic runes link it with the elk, a giant deer or moose that dwelt in the wetlands.

The runestave can be seen as the grass, the antlers of the elk, or its wide splayed toes carrying it over mud. The stave can also be a bird's footprint in the mud, a trident for catching fish, or a swan in flight. All these images reinforce the watery environment that EOLHX calls to mind. Swamplands and marshes are neither land nor water. They present difficult terrain that can be treacherous to those who are unfamiliar with safe pathways and the means to survive there. The core meaning of the rune is protection from harm – not by strong attack or defence as in other runes, but by knowledge of one's surroundings. The hunter will catch the elk or the fish only by blending in with surroundings so well that the prey is not startled away. EOLHX represents effective invisibility together with knowledge of the world and, through this combination, ultimate success in achieving one's goals.

Far right: EOLHX represents protection from harm; new positive influences and trust.

Below: Germanic runes link EOLHX with the elk.

The power and strength of the natural world inherent in the rune energy of EOLHX carries also the presence of the Earth Goddess – the ultimate protector of all living things. This rune is one of the most powerful protections from harm. It indicates the support of the Earth Goddess herself and, with that, success in all ventures.

EOLHX: elk, eel-sedge, protection.

Protection from harm; new positive influences; friendship; trust; expansion of life; optimism; harmony with surroundings Reversed: danger through ignorance; vulnerability; naivety; greed; gullibility; lack of sensitivity.

SIGEL is the last rune of the second aett. Its letter is 'S' and its meaning is 'sun'. Its oldest root words 'sawel', 'swen', 'sun', all refer to the sun, whilst 'sige', is victory and 'sigle' is a jewel or treasure. The runestave represents the force of life and light: sunbeams breaking through cloudbanks; lightning piercing the darkness; the spinning sun disc; or the prehistoric symbol of the svastika or fylfot – all can be seen in the runestave.

SIGEL represents the ability of life-energy to overcome all obstacles and so can mean physical health and well-being. In the *Anglo-Saxon Rune Poem* the sun is a beacon of hope and a guide to those who sail upon the sea. The idea of guidance and spiritual leadership is present in SIGEL. The energy of the sun, fire and lightning is beneficial where it remains balanced, but in an unbalanced state, where energy is already high, SIGEL can signify nervous exhaustion, burn-out, egomania and loss of perspective.

Below: SIGEL is the last rune of the second aett. Its letter is 'S' and its meaning is 'sun'.

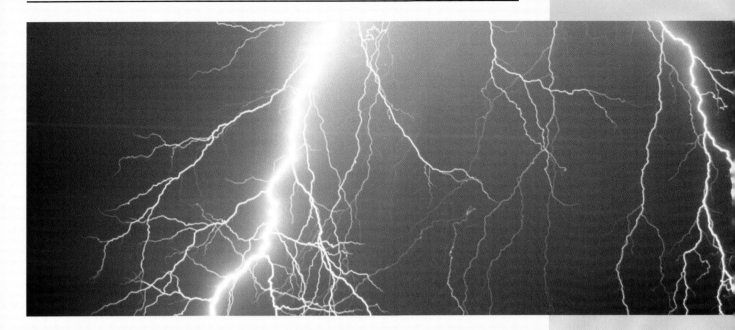

SIGEL is one of the commonest runes inscribed on swords of the Dark Ages. It invokes the power of victory, success and unstoppable energy. Although the sun is associated with the gentle, invulnerable god Baldur 'the Bright', it is the lightning bolt of the giant god Thor which is more readily associated with SIGEL.

SIGEL brings a dynamic force to a divination reading. As the sun can break through dark clouds and lightning can illuminate the night, SIGEL activates everything around it.

SIGEL: sun, success.

Health; energy to be used wisely; wise direction; success; victory; activation; spiritual direction or illumination.

The second aett is sometimes called Heimdall's aett. Heimdall is the doorkeeper and watcher of the gods who dwells on the Rainbow Bridge, Bifrost, that links the earth to the upper worlds. In this aett, five out of the eight runestaves are non-reversible: whichever way up they appear their visual form remains the same. All runes in this aett have symmetry of reflection or rotation – they are dynamic, yet the movement is always about a stable axis point. Primal energies – hail, ice, time, sun, earth are the focus of this aett.

Above: the lightning bolt of the giant god Thor is more readily associated with SIGEL.

TIR, pronounced 'tear', is the first rune of the third aett. Its letter is 'T' and it represents a specific deity: the ancient sky-god Tyr, Tiu, Tiw, Tiwaz, Taranis or Teutates. TIR is related in energy and origin to the Greek Zeus. Both derive from the Indo-European root word 'deiw...', 'sky-god', 'heaven', 'shining one'.

In the *Anglo-Saxon Rune Poem* TIR is equated with the guidance of the Pole Star which 'never fails'. The runestave itself represents a nail, arrow or pointer. It can be seen as a balance, for TIR, although a warrior god, also represented the force of justice, honesty and courage. TIR relates to doing the right thing regardless of personal wishes – like the compass needle that can only ever point to the true North of the Pole Star: TIR can only act to maintain cosmic balance.

Below: TIR, pronounced 'tear', is the first rune of the third aett.

In order to subdue the ravaging demon-wolf Fenris, the gods asked the dwarves to make unbreakable bonds. These were so thin and fragile-looking that Fenris became suspicious when taunted to try them on. He would only agree if a god placed a hand in his mouth. Tyr did this but, as Fenris struggled to get free, the bonds became tighter and he bit off Tyr's hand. The runestave can be seen as Tyr's arm (the upright line) between the jaws of Fenris the wolf (the enclosing V-shape).

Magically, TIR is found frequently on spear and sword blades – true aim, true mark, balance, bravery.

In divination, TIR often appears when truth is an issue or when legalities or judgement are necessary. Honesty and courage will be needed to ensure success. TIR is also a motivating, activating energy. It points the way forward, but in order to get anywhere it must be followed. Navigation through difficult currents and hidden obstacles requires sharp focus on the compass at all times.

In a reading to do with relationships TIR can sometimes represent a powerful male energy or male sexuality.

TIR: star, the god Tyr, courage.

Tenacity; motivation; increase in wealth and power; justice; positive balance
Reversed: lack of energy; impatience; failure; injustice.

Above: TIR often appears when truth is an issue or when legalities or judgement are necessary.

BEORC is the second rune of the third aett. It is the birch tree and the letter 'B'. BEORC can be seen as a mother's breasts, nurturing and protecting, or as a pregnant woman with breasts and big belly. The rune is the main representation of the Mother Goddess and so shows every aspect of creativity, bringing forth, giving birth and nurturing.

As well as representing the energy of the Goddess, BEORC is a tree rune – though the species varies from source to source. In the *Anglo-Saxon Rune Poem* the verse is more suggestive of a poplar than a birch, whilst in the *Icelandic Rune Poem*, a fir tree is named.

Linguistically and conceptually, however, the most appropriate tree for BEORC is the birch. The name derives from the same root words as

Right: BEORC can represent a mother's breasts, nurturing and protecting.

Far right: the most appropriate tree for BEORC is the birch.

'to shine', 'bright', 'white', and also 'to carry' or 'bear'. Some also believe there is a connection with concepts of protection and hiding as in the Old English 'beorgan', to protect, and words like 'beoch' – protected hill and barrow (both in the sense of basket and enclosed burial chamber). The Spring Goddess of light and fertility in Celtic Ireland, Brigid or Bride, also derives from the same root words 'bright' and 'exalted'.

BEORC can represent a mother figure or a woman in a reading, but more generally will be the creative process. BEORC is the rune of beginnings and new starts. This can be the very first stages of an idea before things become clear or it can be the combination of the creative process in overseeing and steering the development of what has been brought forth. In this respect BEORC can sometimes represent children.

Magically, BEORC refers to women's health, particularly fertility. BEORC is also used to bring the energies of the Mother Goddess into full play.

BEORC: birch tree, growth.

Generation; new beginning; birth; a tangible result; endless expansion; family; mother
Reversed: family problems; friction; disputes; misfortunes; loss of creative energy.

Right: the horse has always been held in high regard in Indo-European cultures.

M EH represents a horse and the letter 'E'. It is the third rune of the third aett. It can be seen as the body of a horse, or two horses touching noses. The horse has always been held in high regard in Indo-European cultures, both as a practical means of travel, work and warfare and also as a spiritual being. Horses were used in divination and very important sacrificial rituals. In India the twin healer-gods, the Ashwins, derive their name from 'ashva'- horse.

The quality of partnership is present in EH. The relationship between mankind and the horse is strong. The horse has made possible travel, conquest, wealth and control for those possessing them. Co-operation between horse and rider makes two species into a powerful new entity. Ancient fertility rituals seem to have been associated with the horse. Both Frey and Freya assumed horse forms and several myths tell of gods shapeshifting into a horse form.

EH is a vehicle, a means to travel, a way to move on. This may represent a physical object like a car or bike, but it can equally refer to travelling in the mind, of journeying to the spirit worlds in meditation or trance.

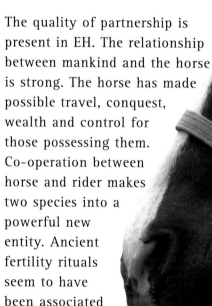

Left: magically, EH refers to the means by which to go wherever we need to go – a spirit horse or magic carpet.

EH also represents our own personal vehicle, the physical body. Where it appears in a health-orientated reading, it will focus attention on how we are treating ourselves. EH brings with it the responsibility of loyalty and trust. Partnerships, 'means to progress onwards', and sometimes brothers and sisters are indicated by this rune.

Magically, EH refers to the means by which to go wherever we need to go – a spirit horse or magic carpet.

EH: horse, movement.

A change for the better; change involving travel; progress; new attitudes; means of travel; partnerships; loyalty; contracts Reversed: unplanned changes; changes for the worse; a long journey; inability to move forward; arguments.

MAN is the fourth rune of the third aett. It means 'mankind' and represents the letter 'M'. The word derives from the Indo-European 'man' and 'manu' that are the roots for words to do with mental activity, like 'mind', 'mental' and 'memory'. The runestave can be seen as two individuals holding each other, the vertical strokes linked together by the relationship and interdependence of the 'X' of GIFU.

The *Anglo-Saxon Rune Poem* links MAN to the strength and co-operation and mutual support between people, though goes on to say that even the strongest bonds are eventually broken by death. The two other rune poems talk of humanity as 'the augmentation of the dust', for in both Christian and pagan cosmology humankind was crafted from the primal earth, breathed upon and brought to life by the Elder gods.

Below: MAN is seen as two individuals holding each other.

The form of MAN is similar to the previous rune, EH, and there is a connection of meaning. Both energies relate to support and help. MAN particularly emphasises the need to realise that support from others is necessary for nearly every activity. It is the mental skills – thought, creativity and memory – that allow us to be more than dust, and it is other people with their support and encouragement that allow us to survive in the world.

Magically, MAN represents the creative will, the imaginative power of the human mind that is able to mould and shape reality any way it chooses. It binds together concepts and energies of a similar nature and creates an orderliness and hierarchy that ensures success.

MAN: mankind, humanity, interdependence.

Co-operation; help, assistance; the rational mind; relatives and supporters; useful contacts; the need for combined action; constructive thought processes. Reversed: self-imposed isolation; obstruction; selfishness; someone from outside the group; destructive tendencies; lack of thought; reckless destructive behaviour.

Above: MAN represents the imaginative power of the human mind that is able to mould and shape reality.

Above: LAGU is the letter 'L' and means lake, water or sea.

Far right: if the force of LAGU is resisted, the build-up of dammed energy will prove destructive like a flood washing away everything before it.

LAGU is the fifth rune of the third aett. It is the letter 'L' and means lake, water or sea. The runestave can be seen as representing the movement of water downwards to the lowest possible level, or as ice (|) melting with the addition of heat (\) and then flowing downhill to the sea. 'Lake', 'leak' and 'loch' all derive from the same root words. Another association with the rune name and its shape is that of the leek. As the earliest fresh green food in Spring, the leek represents the force of life and is said to have been the first plant to re-appear after the Flood. The leek was added to sacrificial drink and was a symbol of power and purification.

All watery qualities are indicated by LAGU – flow, fluidity, and the necessity of water for life to continue – hence life-force. Psychic sensitivity, intuition, the watery flow of feelings and emotional tides are also suggested by LAGU. The power of the emotions, the instincts and the unconscious mind are also under this rune's influence.

The flow of LAGU can be a strong help in all situations where movement, growth and increase are required. However, if its force is resisted the build-up of dammed energy will very often prove destructive, like a flood washing away everything before it.

Magically, LAGU indicates a dynamic thrust to all flows of energy, releasing and directing, and acting as a channel or riverbed to other forces.

LAGU: water, intuition.

Fluidity; intuition; psychic abilities; inspiration; source of all life; journey over water; life-force; strong feelings. Reversed: confused thoughts and feelings; wrong decisions; lack of creativity; neurosis.

ING means the god Ing or Ingvi, and is related to the concept of bright light or a beacon. It has been directly linked by some scholars to the star Arcturus, one of the harbingers of Spring in the northern hemisphere. Its letter is the 'NG' sound and it is the sixth rune of the third aett.

In Anglo-Saxon, 'ing' was used to denote 'son of', 'offspring from', generalised to 'people of', and so is related directly to fertility and generation. ING is an aspect of the major god of fertility, Frey, 'The Lord'. The runestave can be seen as a seed that has sprouted, or even as the double helix of DNA. ING has an alternative form of a simple diamond, or as a diamond resting upon a single vertical stroke. These again can be interpreted as seeds or genitalia, both male and female

Below: the runestave of ING can be seen as the double helix of DNA.

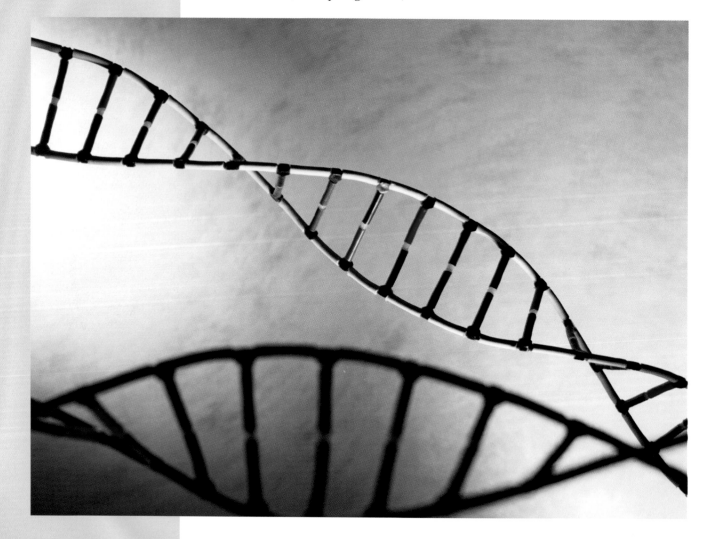

The runestave has no vertical components in its commonest form, indicating great dynamism and movement that are nonetheless balanced around an invisible central axis. This axis is the hidden potential whose creativity is also revealed in its form of two interconnected CENs (<) or one GIFU on top of another.

ING is the seed of things, the dreams and plans that spur us to action, and it is the energy to make these things succeed and flourish. Although a rune of beginnings, it is also a sign of successful completion, fulfilment and harmony. ING reflects the positive benevolence of a light-bringing god of harmony and the fertility of the world, caring for his descendants, offspring or followers.

ING shows all conditions are ripe for fulfilment in whatever area of a reading it appears. In a spiritual context this rune represents the balanced, enlightened human being successfully reaching their full potential.

Magically, ING relates to successful and positive conclusion and creativity made manifest. ING can also refer to sexual energy.

ING: the god Ingvi, beacon.

Realisation of a dream; successful conclusions; inner harmony; relief; freedom from worry and anxiety; important stages of life.

Above: ING is the seed of things, the dreams and plans that spur us to action.

ETHEL, or OTHEL, is the seventh rune of the third aett. The meaning is 'homeland' and the sound is 'OE'. This rune is the 23rd in the *Anglo-Saxon Rune Poem,* but in some other rune rows it is placed 24th. In this text ETHEL is defined as the land where one can remain surrounded by the prosperity of one's possessions. The runestave can be said to resemble the ground plan of a building or farm enclosure, or else it could be seen as a precious ring, brooch or other heirloom.

The meaning of ETHEL will vary depending on context. Very often in divination ETHEL represents the home, the physical dwelling place. Because it also carries the concept of continuity ETHEL may also represent family possessions and inherited property. In more general terms ETHEL is the place, not necessarily physical, where a person feels most 'at home', where the sense of belonging is complete. ETHEL can thus be a sacred space or a state of mind. The rune shape returns on itself, like the past returning into the future through the present moment. Sometimes ETHEL can refer to memory – bringing things forward from the past – remembering, reliving, reinstating what has been.

Below: the runestave of ETHEL can be said to resemble the ground plan of a building or farm enclosure,

Unlike FEOH, ETHEL does not represent exchange or economic activity. The flow is not outwards in ETHEL but self-contained and cyclical. It has the feeling of being rooted through time and place and so can be seen as containing the energies of the land. ETHEL is contentment, security and belonging. It is integrity and a safe place.

Magically, ETHEL suggests ground-edness, centredness and the protection of an established space. It can mean a quiet, safe, hidden space in which to work or refer to the energies of the Earth and the past.

ETHEL: homestead.

Properties; heirlooms; culmination and establishment of a stage of development; return home; inherited traditions and possessions; persistence; continuity; prestige; memory; re-consideration; re-examination of the past.
Reversed: delay; frustration; impatience; needing to stand alone; insecurity; loss of identity; confusion; inaccurate memories; problems inherited from the past or family.

Below: ETHEL reversed can suggest insecurity; loss of identity; confusion.

DAG is 'day'. It is the eighth rune of the third aett, the 24th rune of the Elder Futhark. Its letter is 'D' and derives from the Indo-European root words for 'day', 'timespan', 'heat' and similar concepts. In both Celtic and Germanic custom a day began and ended with sunset. The form of the DAG runestave represents the two halves of the day – the night followed by the daylight hours. By starting the 'day' at dusk the first activities are relaxation, feasting and enjoyment, followed by sleep and then work as the sun rises. DAG carries this theme for, although it represents turning points and times of transformation, its underlying mood is one of optimism and successful conclusions.

The *Anglo-Saxon Rune Poem*, taking a Christian influenced world-view, emphasises the 'glorious light of the Creator', which shines on all and benefits all creatures alike. More specifically, DAG's energy is the energy of the turning point, where one phase of activity has reached its height and is about to transform into another. Midday, midnight, the seasonal changes at solstice and equinox are all aspects of DAG.

Below: in both Germanic and Celtic custom a day began and ended with sunset.

Left: DAG energy encompasses and balances all extremes.

In this respect DAG represents a doorway – and the word 'door' itself derives from closely related root words. Magically, DAG is one of the main runes of protection. As a doorway it allows through beneficial and harmless energies, but acts as an effective barrier to all damaging influences. DAG refers to bringing matters to a climax, after which opposite qualities will begin to gain the ascendancy.

DAG is the sign for wholeness, from one extreme to the other, from darkness to light. Its energy encompasses and balances all extremes yet it implies that once something is completed there must be change into some other state.

DAG: day, balance.

Dawn of a new day; new start; completion; increase; growth; new experiences; prosperity; optimism; change of mind; a shift from one state to another; positivity; balance; transformation.

Below and right: the fourth aett begins with AC, the oak tree.

The third aett is the aett of Tyr. All runes here except one (LAGU) have a vertical axis of symmetry. Four runes, MAN, ING, ETHEL and DAG, contain one or more GIFU (X) runes, emphasising the energy of relationship, exchange, mutuality.

Five runes, BEORC, MAN, ING, ETHEL and DAG, have enclosed spaces, while the remaining three are open and linear. From this simple analysis of shape, it appears that this aett reflects the energy of TIR: balance is the theme, both internally (MAN, ING, DAG) and with the fertilising energies of the world (BEORC, ING, LAGU, DAG).

The fourth, Anglo-Saxon and British Northumbrian, aett begins with AC, the oak tree. Its sound is 'A'. This rune is one of the five in the extended rune row named after trees.

The *Rune Poem* describes some of the main functions of the oak tree for mankind. Its fruit, the acorn, was a major source of food for pigs, its wood the primary boat-building material. The poet sees the ocean as a test for the 'honourable faith' of the wood.

The runestave itself can be seen as a combination of CEN with SIGEL, creative fire meeting the power of the sun or the lightning bolt. Oak trees have a long association with lightning, their deep taproots acting as an effective grounding for the forces of the thunderstorm. This observation naturally links the tree with storm and thunder deities. In the North this meant Thor, the dependable protector of gods and mankind.

Above: oak trees have a long association with lightning which naturally links the tree with storm and thunder deities.

Far right: the ash tree is usually thought of as being the World-Tree.

Below: like the fruit of the oak, AC holds a lot of energy stored within it.

The divination meaning of AC relates to the well-known properties of the tree: strength, durability and slow but dependable growth. AC refers to great capacity for development, but patience is required whenever it appears in a reading. It may suggest trying times are ahead that will test the 'honourable faith' of the questioner. However, the ability to come through all problems is also indicated.

Magically, AC suggests the steady increase of power, a controlled build-up of fire and earth energy that will release when the time is appropriate. Like the fruit of the oak (the acorn), the rune holds a lot of energy stored within it that can be sustaining to growth over a long time.

AC: oak tree, steady growth.

Slow and steady growth; dependability; perseverance; ability to manifest practical energy; endurance.
Reversed: lack of foresight; impatience; unreliability; unstable energy

AESC, pronounced 'ash', is the second rune of the fourth aett. It is the ash tree and has the sound value of 'AE'. The runestave takes the form of the fourth rune AS, in the Germanic Futhark, which in the Anglo-Saxon runes has become OS. The divinatory meaning is quite similar to that of the fourth rune, except that here there is a distinction to be made between different levels of learning, different levels of teaching, and the quality of communication. AESC indicates that a more subtle, spiritual, non-ordinary level of communication is taking place.

The ash tree is usually thought of as being the World-Tree, Yggdrassil, that supports and maintains all the levels of existence from the lower worlds to the highest of heavens. In fact, the original World-Tree was probably what we now call the rowan or else a yew tree.

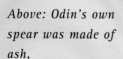

Above: Odin's own spear was made of ash,

Far right: YR represents a war-axe or war-hammer.

Ash and elm were the trees from which the gods formed the first man and woman respectively and, despite its physical appearance with light grey bark and airy canopy, ash is connected with many male activities, particularly warfare. The shaft of Odin's own spear was made of ash, as were the spear shafts and bows of mortal warriors. Ash wood has the greatest weight-bearing flexibility of any wood which made it an invaluable building material.

Magically, AESC relates to the passageways along the roots and branches of the World-Tree which enable information to reach our awareness from other realms. It suggests strength and flexibility to be able to contain and make use of this influx of spiritual energy and power.

AESC: the ash tree, high communication.

Similar to OS, except AESC is at a finer level; subtle intuition; inspiration from other realms; contact with one's highest self or spiritual teachers; influx of spiritual energies; ability to work with many different levels of energy in a practical way. Reversed: confusions of thought, ideas and messages; false information; deception; failure of understanding; inability to handle subtle energies effectively.

YR is the third rune of the fourth aett. It has been interpreted as 'bow' and the letter 'Y'. The exact meaning of the rune-name is not, however, at all clear. Some commentators consider that YR is a saddle or another kind of accoutrement for horses, or a war-axe or war-hammer. Whatever the exact linguistic meaning, the runestave and core concepts enable a useable and useful interpretation of YR's energy.

YR refers to an artefact, a carefully designed tool that combines many different elements. A bow consists of wood and sinew, the arrows of wood, metal, bird's feathers and sinew. Animal, vegetable and mineral kingdoms have all been used, skilfully brought together and melded harmoniously to create an effective, efficient weapon that is a 'joy to princes and nobles'. YR represents the creative skills of mankind – the ability to combine very different things that have no apparent connection to bring into existence a new thing.

Below: YR is a bow under tension. Its great energy is held focused and motionless.

As a bow, the runestave for YR is clearly representative. The arch of UR is the bent bow, the line IS (|) is the arrow. So YR is a bow under tension. Its great energy is held focused and motionless, ready to speed to its target. The UR rune suggests great, natural, barely containable life-force and vitality, whilst the IS rune denotes stillness, frozen time, utmost focus. YR brings together these two polarities of dynamism and control.

Magically, YR has a quality of protection from harm. This arises from its ability to bring intellect and strength together to solve all difficulties and remove obstacles by skill.

YR: bow, synthesis.

Focusing of skills; synthesis of ideas and practices; control; concentration on goals; one-pointedness; drawing together. Reversed: aimless; clumsiness; lack of focus; lack of control and poor understanding.

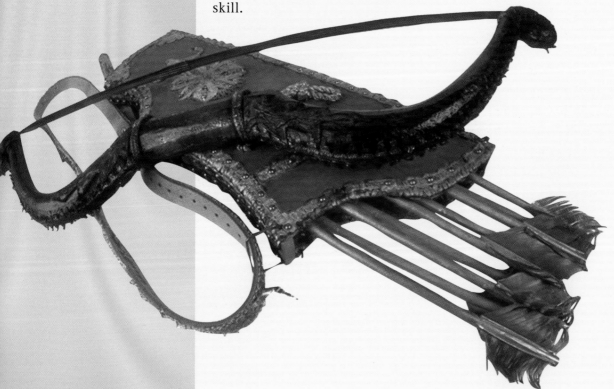

IOR or IAR, pronounced 'ee-aar', is the fourth rune of the fourth aett. Its sound is 'IO' or 'ia' and in the *Anglo-Saxon Rune Poem* it is referred to as a 'river-fish'. Because the rune poem goes on to describe a beast that feeds on land yet lives happily surrounded by water, many have considered IOR to represent the beaver or otter – both considered as 'fish' in medieval times. Others believe IOR to represent a sea-snake or sea-monster associated with the World-Serpent Jörmungand. Both meanings add to the richness of the rune's interpretation.

The beaver and otter exhibit similar qualities. Both are equally happy living on land or in the water. Few other creatures can be seen to happily dwell in two worlds simultaneously. IOR thus represents the energy of flexibility and the ability to carry on despite what the surrounding conditions might be.

Below: the rune poem goes on to describe a beast that feeds on land yet lives happily surrounded by water, many have considered IOR to represent the beaver or otter.

Above: the World-Serpent, Jörmungand, forms the surrounding boundary of Middle Earth.

The World-Serpent, Jörmungand, forms the surrounding boundary of Middle Earth on the outer limits of the World-Ocean. It lies underneath the solid earth and continually gnaws the roots of Yggdrassil, the World-Tree. Because it would rise up with the rest of primal forces to fight the gods in the Last Battle, Thor one day decided to go out in a boat and catch the monster on his fishing line. Having succeeded in catching the monster, he eventually had to cut the line because the titanic struggle was in danger of destroying the world itself. Although perceived as a negative or evil force, the World-Serpent was part of the inherent duality maintaining existence. To slay it would disturb cosmic balance.

IOR is the ability to see extremes in the world yet remain unaffected or non-attached. Like the beaver, IOR invites you to exist in whatever world you find yourself in and yet remain happy and content. Where IOR appears in a reading it often indicates that the questioner is becoming burdened by the apparent evil and troubles of the world and wishes to do more, or feels guilty about not doing more. These situations are beyond the individual's ability to alter and, in reality, may be more a problem of belief systems and personal perception, than intrinsically 'evil'.

The runestave is almost identical to the snowflake variation of the HAEGL rune, suggesting the theme of cosmic forces in balance. The form of IOR could be remembered as NYD negated, summing up the theme of 'no need'; 'don't worry', 'action isn't necessary', 'learn to accept', and so on.
Magically, IOR refers to balance amidst polarity

IOR: beaver, sea-monster, non-attachment.

Acceptance of apparent evil and negativity; don't try to change what cannot be changed; living happily under all sorts of conditions; non-attachment to value judgements; equanimity

Above: IOR invites you to exist in whatever world you find yourself in and yet remain happy and content.

EAR is the fifth rune of the fourth aett. Its sound value is 'EA' and its meaning is 'dust' or 'earth' in its original meaning of 'the grave'. The Indo-European root word is 'er-', earth or ground. The shape of the runestave resembles the Irminsul – the ritual pillar that holds heaven and earth in place. This world axis, repeated in the main supporting column of the chief's hall, was sacred to a god named Ir or Er.

The *Rune Poem* describes EAR as the dust of the grave to which all mankind returns. It is certainly a rune of endings, but is not necessarily a negative situation. To maintain the balance of heaven and earth, things must continually change, and death is simply a change from one energy state to another, leading to new beginnings. In order to survive, organisms must consume other organisms. Death, then, is at the very heart of life.

Below: the Rune Poem describes EAR as the dust of the grave.

Dust is the finest visible particles of matter. EAR, in a rune reading, often suggests that, although things may appear to have fallen apart in a final dissolution, something still exists that can be constructively worked upon.

Magically, EAR relates to dissolving energy or bringing together scattered elements into a new form of power.

EAR: dust, collapse.

Endings; things falling apart; dissolution; looking beyond apparent death or collapse to the finest level of activity still going on; examine every issue including the insignificant; the lesson that everything ends, but energy is eternal – look somewhere else.
Reversed: failure to examine all options; apparent failure; uselessness; fear of death and endings.

Above: EAR, in a rune reading, often suggests that, although things may appear to have fallen apart in a final dissolution, something still exists that can be constructively worked upon.

CWEORTH is the sixth rune of the fourth aett. Its name means 'sacred fire' and its letter is 'Q' (cw). This form of the runestave has been chosen rather than alternatives that could be easily confused with EAR.

CWEORTH is the altar fire, the sacrificial fire that transforms offerings into a form that becomes food for the gods, spirits and ancestors. Its key theme is therefore transformation. The runestave can be seen as two CENs (<): one lower, earthbound fire transformed by the focus of place (|), the altar, into an upper, celestial spiritual fire. SIGEL and EOH are also echoed in CWEORTH's form. CWEORTH is the fire of creativity that rapidly consumes what has been to release what is to come. To human beings change can be one of the most

Below: CWEORTH is the altar fire, the sacrificial fire that transforms offerings into food for the gods, spirits and ancestors.

painful of experiences, especially when it is sudden and complete. CWEORTH, whenever it appears, indicates times of rapid change and growth that ultimately will prove completely necessary and beneficial, but may be a little rough while the process is underway.

In the context of a loss of some sort, CWEORTH shows that more shall be gained in the future. Within a spiritual context, CWEORTH can mean a powerful transformative experience, or the need to carry out actions that have spiritual, rather than material significance.

Magically, CWEORTH suggests the cleansing, purifying fire of offering that allows shifts of awareness and new clarity of consciousness. It is an energy of transmutation and spiritualisation.

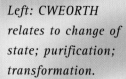

Left: CWEORTH relates to change of state; purification; transformation.

CWEORTH: sacred fire, transformation.

Ritual actions that bring about a change of state; purification; transformation; rapid change; spiritual growth; transformative experiences; sacrifice (offering up something important in order to receive more).

Right: as a chalice, or offering cup, CALC is the vessel that enables human beings to communicate with the spirit realms.

CALC is the seventh rune of the fourth aett. Its meaning is uncertain. It may mean 'chalk' or 'chalice'. It has the sound of a hard 'K'. As a chalice, or offering cup, CALC is the vessel that enables human beings to communicate with the spirit realms. The qualities of chalk link it visually to the bones of the dead or the bones of the earth itself. This suggests that CALC may represent the act of making offerings, via the earth, to the spirits of the ancestors – a widespread and universal practice among native peoples.

Whilst EAR suggests the dissolution of physical matter and CWEORTH suggests matter to be transformed into spirit food for the gods, CALC refers to blessings and nourishment for the ancestors. CALC can be seen as an upturned cup resting on the earth. It can also represent tree-roots, which is a fitting symbol for the progenitors, those ancestors who have gone before us and to whose existence we owe our own lives and knowledge.

CALC represents the underlying vitality that supports us – the continuity with the past and the appreciation of the wealth of experience coming down to us from the past. In a divination, CALC often indicates getting back to basics. It suggests looking back to the past or to the beginning of a situation. CALC can represent the ancestors of the questioner, either those in the distant past, or parents and grandparents.

Magically, CALC refers to the genetic and spiritual forebears whose skill and knowledge underlie our own. It represents a conduit for communication between the physical and the spiritual realms.

CALC: chalice, chalk, roots.

The time to look at one's core needs; the deepest aspect of any situation; a source of strength; talking with one's ancestors; the Unconscious; what is not apparent; the hidden source. Reversed: topsy-turvy attitudes; lack of practicality; failure to examine true motives; rejection of the source of sustenance; egotism.

Above: CALC represents ancestors, either those in the distant past, or parents and grandparents.

Below: the STAN runestave can be seen as a stone – a carved block or boulder or as a gaming piece.

STAN is the eighth rune of the fourth aett. It means 'stone' and has the sound value of 'ST' The Indo-European root 'sta' is still found in many English words. It signifies the concept of stability and standing, of firm endurance over time and of strength. The runestave can be seen as a stone – a carved block or boulder or as a gaming piece carved from stone or bone. STAN can also suggest the clarity and precision of crystal: the most noble and precious form of stone. As a hewn rock STAN can be an altar stone, the centrepiece of ritual and ceremony.

STAN can represent a solid wall, a block that prevents all forward movement, or it can represent a cave mouth in a cliff, or a megalith or crystal, a doorway to experiencing other realms and realities.

STAN represents the uncompromising reality of the world, which also ironically is the gateway to all mysteries and transcendence of the physical. The runestave is like an EH mirroring itself as if it were a self-contained vehicle to move between worlds. STAN also looks like a PEORTH joined or contained by IS – that is, potential creativity, or the numinous presence of creation, become crystallised and solidified.

Left: magically, STAN contains the secrets of the universe as if it was a crystal ball – and possesses the organising power of crystal, too.

Magically, STAN suggests a protective barrier, a safe, strong place upon which to stand. It contains the secrets of the universe as if it was a crystal ball – and possesses the organising power of crystal, too.

STAN: stone, altar, standing stone, stability.

Solidity; strength; entrance, or blocked doorway, to other levels; restrained energy; waiting; the bones or support of a situation; crystallisation; the still centre; a power place.

The fourth aett begins with dynamic, non-symmetrical runestaves – AC, AESC and YR – while the remaining runes all have axes of symmetry – a sign of stable and unchanging qualities of energy. Three of these runes – IAR, CWEORTH and STAN – are non-reversible, showing that there is an inherent core quality that goes beyond opposites or polarity. There seems to be an emphasis on understanding fundamental principles in order to further spiritual understanding. Oak, ash, death, stone, earth – each one can act as a gateway to powerful living and spiritual awakening.

DEVELOPING DIVINATION SKILLS

Far right: in order to tune into the questioner's situation, it is a good idea always to start with a general reading that gives you an overview of that person's life.

GETTING THE SETTING CORRECT

All divination depends on the ability of the reader to enter a state of awareness that is somewhat outside of the flow of normal time and space. This 'in-between' state is felt as an emotional and mental neutrality where the patterns and pictures of the oracle form meaningful relationships and 'speak' to the reader. To reach this state each person will find their own helpful patterns of behaviour. Sometimes it might be as simple as lighting a candle or some incense, or perhaps wearing particular jewellery or surrounding yourself with spiritually significant items. Having a set procedure of preparation can begin to trigger the necessary altered state. Draw a rune from your bag or pack to determine whether you are ready to proceed. If the energy does not feel quite right, it is possible to draw out one or two runes intuitively that, as you imagine their energies enter your surroundings, will induce the required clarity and calm.

TYPES OF READING

How you begin a reading will often depend upon the nature of the questions. It is a good idea to make clear that a rune divination is not mind-reading nor clairvoyance, nor is it a test of your cleverness at guessing. If you, as the reader, need clarification on a point or verification that you are seeing the right patterns, the questioner should be willing to offer accurate information. In order to tune into the questioner's situation it is a good idea to always start with a general reading that gives you an overview of that person's life. Important issues will begin to emerge from this that can be explored later in detailed readings. The accuracy of a general reading will give the reader confidence to go into more detail, and gives the questioner a chance to see how the process works.

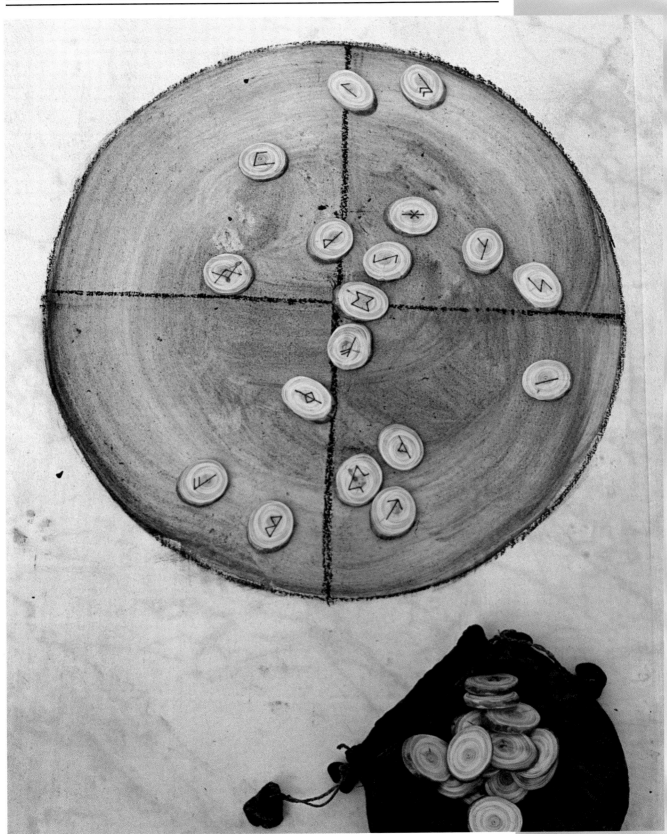

The questioner themselves knows their situation best, and also usually has a good idea of the possible options that are open to them. Thus, allowing the questioner to select, choose or throw the runes for themselves means that whatever reading arises it has been their energy involved rather than your own. Simply ensure that both of you are clear about the intention of each rune cast before any runes are selected. You, as reader, will need to hold in your mind the number of runes that will be drawn and, if you are using a set pattern, what each placement is going to signify. As the questioner picks out each rune ask that it is either laid down on the table or given to you so that it can be placed appropriately into the layout. This will be particularly important when taking reversed positions of runes into account. If a casting method is being used, have the question very clearly in mind and continue to shake the bag of runes gently until it feels right to cast them onto the reading surface.

Casting Patterns

One of the simplest casting patterns is a circle divided into four quarters by an equal-armed cross. The horizontal axis represents the flow of time with the past on the left and the future on the right. Runes falling to the left are energies of the past, those around the centre show the current situation, those towards the right show what energies are approaching the questioner.

Below: one of the simplest casting patterns is a circle divided into four quarters by an equal-armed cross.

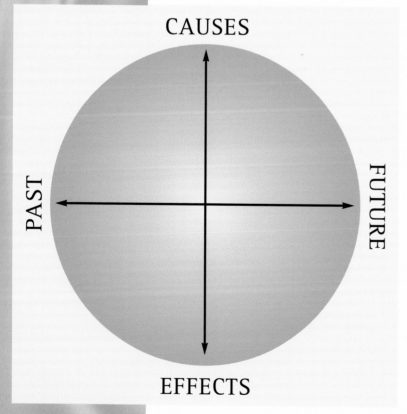

CAUSES

PAST

FUTURE

EFFECTS

The vertical axis represents the movement of energies from potential or subtle spiritual influences at the top, towards manifesting, physical effects at the base of the line. Thus, runes falling in the top half of the circle show hidden causes, or situations that might appear at some time, while those falling closer to the base indicate energies that can be seen working in the physical world.

Another simple casting pattern divides the space into three areas for the past, present and future or, alternatively, the physical, emotional and mental states. The innermost area can be the physical condition or the situation in the past. The second area covers the present situation or the emotions. The outermost section shows future trends or the mental aspects of the reading.

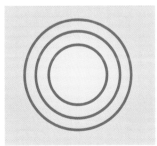
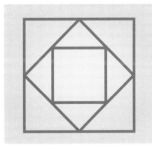
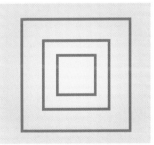

Left: other casting patterns divide the space into three areas for the past, present and future or, alternatively, the physical, emotional and mental states.

Right: when casting methods are used, a decision must be taken as to how to read each rune as it falls.

When casting methods are used, a decision must be taken as to how to read each rune as it falls. Commonly, only those runes that land face upwards are considered as relevant to the question. The reader should decide whether reversed runes are to be read as such, and, if they are, will runes on their side therefore indicate neutral influences, upright runes positive aspects and reversed, difficult aspects? This can sometimes offer a useful comparison of positive and negative qualities surrounding the issue in question.

The same casting pattern can be used to indicate the general situation with an initial rune cast followed up, if necessary, by a more detailed examination of one or more aspects. Simply bear the question firmly in mind before the cast is made.

Notice how the runes fall. Runes that fall close together will be related to the same issue and can be read as a single aspect of the question. Allow your gaze to wander over the pattern of the runes. Links, associations and sequences will suggest themselves to your intuitive state of awareness. Follow the patterns where they seem to be going and clarify with the questioner that what you are seeing makes sense in terms of what they know about the situation.

ᚠᚢᚦᚨᚱᚲᚷᚹᚺᚾᛁᛃᛇᛈᛉᛊᛏᛒᛖᛗᛚᛜᛟᛞ ᚠᚢᚦᚨᚱᚲᚷᚹᚺᚾᛁᛃ

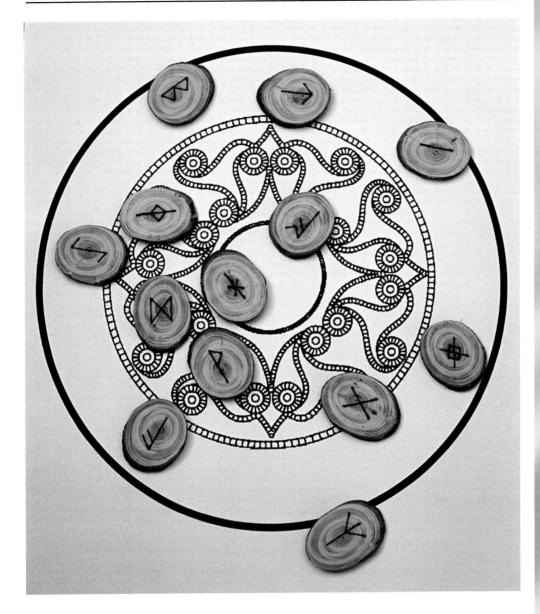

Notice when your gaze continually falls on one area of the cast or on one rune in particular. This usually indicates an important factor or that some more needs to be said about that rune.

Make a note of areas that are not easy to interpret or where more information is needed. Once a cast has been fully explored, another cast can be made to clarify those difficult parts of the reading.

DEVELOPING DIVINATION SKILLS

Right: use a particular placement of 11 runes in a rectangular shape to give an initial reading.

LAYOUT PATTERNS

An excellent pattern to give an initial reading or a detailed answer uses a particular placement of 11 runes in a rectangular shape. Three runes are placed in a vertical line on the left, three on the right. Two runes are placed making a top and bottom row and a final rune is put in the centre. This central rune is examined first as it reveals the main energy or central issue of the reading. The three runes on the left show the personal energies of the questioner. The three opposite show the people around the questioner or their current situation. The whole of the lower row gives an indication of how matters are progressing, whilst the whole of the top row shows the likely outcome.

LAYOUT OF NINE

To expand the simple three-rune layout of past, present and future, a layout of nine can be used. This simple square can be read in many different ways, from top to bottom, from left to right or as an expansion and contraction from start to conclusion diagonally.

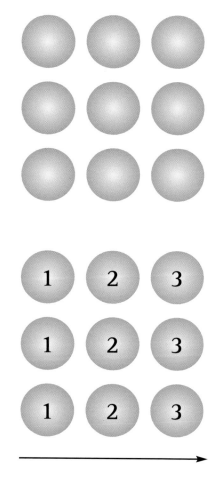

Reading

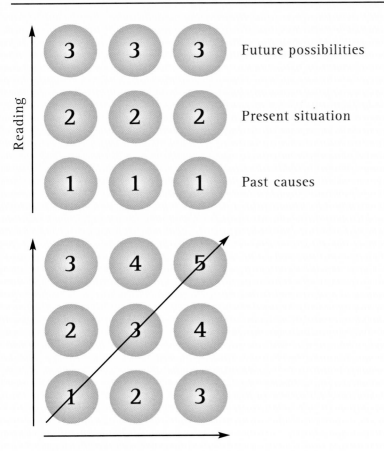

3 3 3   Future possibilities

2 2 2   Present situation

1 1 1   Past causes

Reading

Left: to expand the simple three-rune layout of past, present and future, a layout of nine can be used.

USING RUNES TO RESOLVE ISSUES

Once a reading has clarified a situation, it is very easy to use runes to encourage a more positive outcome. This is because the runes and the shapes of the runestaves themselves have a strong resonance with the universal energies they represent.

Looking at the rune shapes, carrying them around and meditating upon the energies that are needed to help will automatically allow those energies to influence someone's life whether they are familiar with the runes or not.

Asking for runes to help a situation and then simply drawing out one or two that 'feel' right in the hand is simple and effective.

INDEX